The Worst Ghost of All

Helena Pielichaty

Illustrated by
Vincent Vigla

OXFORD
UNIVERSITY PRESS

This is Mr Spit. He sells houses. He is good at selling houses.
"I can sell houses in my sleep!" he brags.

But there is one house he cannot
sell.

It is called High House. It has a lot of rooms. But some of the rooms are cold because...

...some of the rooms are haunted.

There is a ghost in the kitchen.
Her name is Smelly Nelly. She died
long, long ago. If you go into the
kitchen...

...she screams at you...

...until your head throbs.

There is a ghost in the sitting room.
Her name is Scary Mary. She died
long, long ago. If you go into the
sitting room...

...she screams at you...

...until your hair falls out.

There is a ghost in the dining room.
His name is Thin Jim. He died long,
long ago. If you go into the dining
room...

...he screams at you...

...until your teeth crack.

There is a ghost in the bedroom.
Her name is Bossy Flossie. She died
long, long ago. If you go into the
bedroom...

...she screams at you...

...until your ears drop off.

There is a ghost in the bathroom.
His name is Nasty Ned. He died
long, long ago. If you go into the
bathroom...

...he screams at you...

...until your eyes pop out.

Mr Spit is fed up. People hate ghosts. He thinks he will never sell High House.

One day a man comes to see Mr
Spit. His name is Lord C Threw.
"I will buy High House," he says in
a deep, creepy voice.

"Do you know about the ghosts?" Mr Spit asks. Lord C Threw nods. "Ghosts don't bother me," he says.

When Lord C Threw goes,
Mr Spit runs round his office.
"Yes!" he shouts, "I have done it!
I have sold High House!"

"Who to?" everyone asks.

"That man, that Lord C Threw."

"What man? We did not see a man.
We just felt very cold."

"But…" says a puzzled Mr Spit,
"but…"

This is High House. It has a lot of rooms. All the rooms are cold because…

…all the rooms are haunted.

There is a ghost
in the kitchen...

...as well as in the
sitting room.

There's a ghost in
the dining room...

...and there's a ghost in the bedroom...

...and bathroom too.

They all died long ago.

Now there is a ghost in the attic.
His name is Lord C Threw. They
say he is the worst ghost of all. Do
not, *do not* go into the attic.

If you do Lord C Threw will scare
you to...

...death!